Poems beyond the Mountain

John Chambers

Joe Chambers
5/10/18

Copyright: John Chambers, 2017.
ISBN: 978-1-9998013-1-1
Published by John Chambers Publishing.
jonniewchambers@gmail.com
Printed by Amadeus Press

for Ho Yan

Tanu

One day an old raccoon said to his son Tanu, that he had now come of age, and it was time for him to seek wisdom. He loved his father very much, so he went along with his wishes and set off on pilgrimage. He washed in the pure waters of the five holy lakes, and traversed picturesque flower filled meadows. He halted for some time at the foot of the Sacred Mountain, and then began its ascent with anticipation. He had heard wonderful tales of those who had found wisdom there. He climbed up through the magic forest. He trekked through two moons and three suns. Eventually he reached the summit, *where the peak kissed the sky, and cloud encircled its pinnacle like a scarf. The air was crystal clear, cold and fresh, potent with imagination. Tanu was feeling weary now because of his days of climbing. His aching heart was beating so fast, because he felt that his dream was so near being realised. But alas, although from the mountain top he could see forever, he couldn't see at all. For wisdom was out of sight, out of reach, and out of mind. Tears obscured his vision. This moment of disappointment almost seemed like the end of life itself. But then, mysteriously out of the enveloping cloud, appeared a sage dressed in long white robes. His* eyes glowed with kindness, his demeanour whispered wisdom. His dark eyes seemed to know every profound thought held hidden, deep within Tanu's thirsty soul. The sage turned to him and said,

"O little one. There is a forever beyond the forever you now see. There is a mountain in Paradise more majestic than the one on which you now stand. There is a golden light more mellow than the moon that you adore. There is a silence more silent than the falling of any leaf. There is a song in the soft breeze that longs to speak to you. There is a joy deeper than the earth, that exceeds any happiness in the world of men. There are words more exquisite than in any holy books revered in temples across this magnificent wide world. My dear Tanu, wisdom is more than one experience, it is a lifelong journey. Wisdom walked before the worlds were made. She will still be walking once this world is dissolved. She has now chosen to be your companion, let her walk with you as and when she chooses. You have searched for wisdom, but it is she that has found you.

Tanu tried to gather the thoughts spinning around in his head. He closed his tired eyes in contemplation. How long he was like this he could not tell, *but it seemed both a moment and a lifetime in his experience. Now when he opened his eyes again, the sage was gone. But wisdom stood right there beside him, more tangible than life itself.*

Thought I saw a king

wading through the speckled trees

shining in the sun

Awesome sapphire sky

winds chilling in open space

like words in silence

White stones on the path

phosphorescent quartz candles

burnished by sunbeams

Blue skies through the rain

rainbows dancing round my feet

sun is painting me

Birches dance in breeze

bluebell peal soaks glade with song

nature drowned in joy

Steel sharp plane cuts true

smoothing timber to silk soft

hands roughened by blame

Faith fragile as frost

mystical as a rainbow

loud like a heartbeat

Black night stars sparkling

but may be the gleam of a

myriad harp strings

Deep soul lights night sky

moon truth revealed in still lake

mirror lies I know

Wind whispers secrets

fragile leaf asks broad oak why

wisdom holds silence

Grasp the thin green blade

before the harvest reaping

or sands will seize time

Thirsty we drank waves

floated on soft yellow sand

melted in pale sky

Noon day sun ablaze

but veiled by incandescence

what is this fire flame

Silver plated lake

dream clouds kiss the mountain tops

tall trees stand in awe

Rain waste wet falls thick
like grey slate smothering breath
long for lemon sun

Wordsworth's footsteps heard

walking words in front of me

poems etched in paths

Thoughts overflowing

words cling to lips like wet glass

silence like sweet wine

Floods devastate town

mud strewn photos weep real tears

life drains through fingers

In one bowl of rice

ten thousand years of sickles

whisper like the wind

Tai Chi Master glides

slicing the air more softly

than a summer breeze

Despite lack of sight

men stumble across wisdom

from beyond the skies

Deeper than oceans

more solid than mountains is

wisdom in the breeze

Reconciling now

will the earth refuse to turn

and the seas stand still

Think I saw the spark

that lit each shining star and

fired earth's flaming sun

Locked in diamonds

is a thousand years of light

just breathless to blaze

Brooding sky coal black

buffeting wind so fearsome

huge trees are afraid

Effulgent chaste sun

feet feel crunchy frost filled grass

bare trees paint sky blue

Stand before mountain

like raindrop beside ocean

feel adoration

Tears form like dew drops

innocents sob in the dark

the lot has fallen

Beyond present pain

there exists a warm soft sea

bathed in summer sun

Touch the silent void

where stars are born to die and

brave men shake with fear

Avenue of oaks

dappled light through faint shadows

like words in poems

Men stand tall like trees

branch and root so strong and sure

frail hearts hang like leaves

A fork in the road

one way leads to a garden

the other is veiled

Godfather's brown eyes

deeper than the China Sea

bathe me with a glance

Choose to be silent

virtue is better than truth

words lighter than air

Mists shroud holy isle

monks once prayed in ancient church

stone walls still tremble

Crackle of pebbles

steep and descending shoreline

night air swathed with sound

Leaf falls on still lake

waiting now for Tsunami

dread roots many fears

Black dog follows me

night too real dawn never comes

bitten by darkness

Warm sun veiled by cloud

surely there but out of reach

like truth to the wise

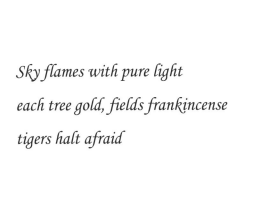

Sky flames with pure light

each tree gold, fields frankincense

tigers halt afraid

Tide waits for its turn

mellow sun waits for new dawn

hearts wait for true love

Bright blue waves beckon

wade in the ocean of life

sink in sentience

Electric blue flash

a kingfisher shocks the air

sky spark from heaven

A glass of water

contains an ocean of stars

swallow galaxies

Walked snow white mountains

sky like buckets of bluebells

intoxicated

Green leaves turn gold now

days are tired nights grow stronger

men brace for winter

I heard a pure voice

in the silent sounds of man

sighs too deep to tell

Two hearts fuse as one

passion waves like autumn leaves

kissing the soft sun

I see pale paper

afraid words might disturb me

ink will not wet page

Walking between worlds

in the land of painted dreams

where soft shadows breathe

Eyes refused to close

we held the sun in our hands

time melted like snow

Warrior stands tired

he has fought beyond fatigue

life can't be beaten

Time buys yesterday

tomorrow is without price

today is pure gold

Champagne setting sun

pouring streams of golden light

across parched meadow

Nature is dancing

ripened corn waves in the breeze

as the earth beats time

.

Forest is opaque

for moments see other worlds

far beyond the trees

Standing on mountain

silenced by sacred landscape

think I see heaven